Tango Obsession

By

JON TARIQ

Thank you to all the people who contributed to this book's enrichment.

Hugs

New York

USA

Dedicated

To all my students past, present, and future.

And to all tango students and tango lovers around the world.

Author's Note:

The information provided in this book is designed to provide helpful information and motivation to its readers. The contents of this book are the sole expression and opinion of its author and are intended to help the reader become a better dancer.

ISBN: 979-8-218-04629-3

New York

USA

A Message from the Author

You will know if you have a tango obsession because you will have an overwhelming desire not just to dance the argentine tango but to have a dance conversation without words with someone. A dance conversation is a great desire to do your best with your improvised moves one tanda (set of 4 consecutive dances) at a time. Sometimes that person is someone you just met and might never see again. Even though you might never see the person again, the memory will stay with you for the rest of your life. And that is where the obsession starts.

Tango is a beautiful, conversational, deeply introspective, flirtatious, impressive, intimate, melancholic, passionate, romantic, and whimsical dance. It is very important to the dancers to want to get better and better at it, but how do they do that?

Commitment, practice, and consistency are extremely important to master any discipline. This is especially true for argentine tango.

Not only will you become a better dancer after reading this book, but you will see significant improvement in your cognitive, emotional, physical, and social well-being.

Tango dance plays a positive multifaceted role in the lives of dancers. It can be used as therapeutic care because it fulfills the need for social contact and improves the level of physical activity.

Tango music is ranked as one of the most pleasurable genres of music. Tango decreases the stress hormone cortisol and helps maintain a sharper and more alert mind, improves balance and posture when dancing as well as in your everyday life, and body image promotes self-esteem and life satisfaction and increases beneficial social interactions. What else can you ask for? Tango is all you need.

The more time you spend practicing argentine tango, the more your body will transform into a perfect vessel for the dance: you will become more agile, and your muscles will get stronger as you learn the language of the tango. But always remember that consistency is the key. If you stop practicing for any significant amount of time, you won't be able to just jump back into it. Like any vehicle left idle, your body and mind won't have adequate power to stay functioning, and the body will slow down. Maintaining peak physical condition and perfecting your technique will become impossible if not practiced regularly. Restart your engine as soon as possible if you stop for a significant time.

Tango passion is a strong and barely controllable emotion that will urge you to do incredible things.

I offer you this book as inspiration to continue your Tango journey.

Welcome!

The history of dance and music goes back thousands of years. There is even evidence of dance in different cave paintings around the world. There are many reasons why human beings have always danced. For us tango dancers, it is for the joy of dancing.

Table of Contents

Steps

Figures!

Embrace!!

Feelings!!!

Connection!!!!!!

Introduction

Argentine tango is a journey that gets the dancer in touch with their soul. During this journey, the dancer discovers different wants and needs, but the direct practice and time spent learning really matter. This happens when a technique is improved, and the dancer understands the dance and its music more fully. The dancer also learns about the dance's unspoken rules (códigos) and how to apply accumulated experience. Finally, when there is an absolute harmony between the dancer, the person they are dancing with, and the music, it soon will or can become an obsession to master its technique.

Tango requires a strong commitment to practice, even to get to a beginner level. However, this discipline of diligent practice will allow you to steadily improve and gradually reach each milestone you set for yourself.

A beginner student should learn all the basic elements such as simple walks, weight shifting, cross-system, parallel system, and terms. Safe dance practice is very important during this time in Tango since It is always possible for beginners to get hurt or hurt someone with their heels while dancing. But this is only possible if they are making the wrong turns while doing embellishments (a decoration for your move). A dancer must learn when, how, and what to do before they attempt any embellishment.

An intermediate student will learn intermediate moves like ocho cortado, cadencia, colgada, volcada, boleos, barridas, sacadas, and ganchos, work on perfecting their basic turns, and many more intermediate-level steps. Students will also learn to be ready to improvise.

Advanced students need more advanced insights on improving posture, difficult combinations, advanced techniques, turns, tempo, and timing. The refining never stops.

Dance is simply the refinement of human movement: walking, running, and jumping. We are all experts. There should be no art form more accessible than dance, but there is no art more baffling to the public imagination.

- Twyla Tharp

If you can walk, you can tango.

- Jon Tariq

Chapter I

What is Tango?

What was it then and what is it now?

What makes Tango so special? Tango is a unique latin dance that differs in so many ways from other dances, from the type of embrace used to the improvisation and passion you develop as you dance it more and more.

Tango has been called both the "Dance of Love" and the "Dance of Sorrow." It is passionate and dramatic because it represents frustrated love. Originally, tango music was a mix of instrumental music, dances and silent theatre.

Origins of tango: then and now:

Tango is a mix of different styles of international dances brought to Argentina by immigrants. Everyone was dancing in their neighborhood, which we call "barrios". There were no formal schools where you could go to learn as you can do today. People will get together in their own barrios and visit different barrios to exchange and compare different ways to dance with each other. This dancing from barrio to barrio is what we call today's dancing club hopping.

Vicenti Rossi, a historian, states that the name tango derives from the Jerga dialect approximately in *1803* and means "tocarse" (to touch). The Jerga dialect was originally the dialect of the lower classes in Argentina. The Argentinian people had at the time a profound sadness and deep resentment toward the millions of immigrants who entered Argentina. They expressed their feelings and emotions through melancholic songs and poems.

Ángel Villoldo (1861-1919) was an argentine musician and poet who is considered "El padre del tango" (The father of Tango) and the most representative artist of the "Vieja Guardia" (Old Guard/Old School/older style). According to an interview made by the newspaper "La Razón" in 1917, we know that he was *a "cuarteador" (In Argentina and Uruguay, the cuarteador was the one who managed a team of horses that pulled a vehicle in mudflats or to climb slopes) in La Calle Larga" de Buenos Aires (The Long Street, today's Montes de Oca) during the time when his interest for music appears, he sang, played the guitar and harmonica. He linked the tango and the gaucho, the two very integral parts of the Argentinian national image.*

In 1899, Argentine violinist Ernesto Ponzio (1885-1934), who they called "el pibe-the kid" publishes and authors the well-known tango "Don Juan", also called "El Taita del barrio" at 13. Because of his father's death, Ernesto had to interrupt his violin studies and go to work performing in canteens and on the streetcars to help his family during hard times. He was asked to play at the most famous places of the time, like "Lo de Hansen" in Buenos Aires, among others. He played the violin "Sacando Chispas" (Extracting Sparks). This tango was the first one recorded with a bandoneon by Vicente Greco and his orchestra in 1910.

Tango dance has been analyzed in so many different ways over the years. Enrique Santos Discelapo, (tango and milonga musician and composer), also known as the "creator of tango, "once said that tango is "a sad thought that is danced."

The Tango was initially prohibited from dancing outside of brothels and bowling alleys and rejected by the upper class and churches as a dance of the lower-class sinners. The dance was unacceptable because of its sexual undertones and the fact that tango often took place in brothels. Later, upper-class writers like Borges, Martinez Estrada, and Mafud o Lugones started to compose Tangos.

Historian Jose Gobello said that candombe, the tango negro (black tango), was born in *1884* and was recognized as the first tango. It was composed by the slave Casimero who was freed from the Amancio Alcorta family. This tango was called "Concha Sucia" (dirty shell). This music piece was recorded in *1917* under the name of "Cara Sucia" (dirty face) by Francisco Canaro and Casimero danced with an Italian dancer by the name of Paulina.

The "Teatro Opera," an opera house in Buenos Aires, 1902 began to include tango music in their Balls. During this time, tango was just one of the many dances practiced locally, but then it became very popular throughout society. The theatres and street barrel organs had a major role in the initial spread from the suburbs to the working-class slums, which were packed with hundreds of thousands of European immigrants.

The german bandoneon instrument (approx. 1850), inspired by the accordion and conceived as a portable version of the harmonium (a type of pump organ), was used in small churches that couldn't afford an organ then. It is believed that german immigrants brought the bandoneon to argentina around 1870. The bandoneon was quickly adopted as part of the tango instrument repertoire because of its dark sound and portability.
The argentinian had the bandoneon with neither maestros nor methods for it. Everything had to be created from scratch. It was like a piece of blank paper on which anything could be written.

1911: The Palais of Glace in Paris theatre presented the Tango by Baron Antonio De Marchi (a noble appointed by the king of England to guard the border between England and Wales, he was also known as the Welsh Marches. An invitation was extended by the Baron to the upper class that were dancing the tango in secret, and they accepted the invitation, and tango was no longer prohibited after that. They danced to a more regulated style than the "tango liso" or simple steps tango and adapted this new version as their own.

1912: Dancers and musicians from Buenos Aires travelled to Europe and the first European tango craze took place in Paris and was soon followed by London, Berlin, and other capitals. The tango debuted in London with a musical show called *Sunshine Girl,* in which the characters danced the tango. Everyone gave an enthusiastic welcome to the dance. After the show, the ladies wanted to learn how to dance, and they organized parties at home to learn. Tango then traveled to Berlin, Rome, Vienna, and so on.

1913: Towards the end of *1913,* it finally made its way to New York and Finland. These exported versions of tango were modified to have less body contact, and still, the tango dance was thought to be shocking by many. During this time, the *Sunshine Girl* show debuted in New York at Radio City Music Hall, and the tango dance and

icon of the tango because tango melodrama portrays a woman who leaves her poor low-class lover for a rich higher, class one. The poor man, "guapo y macho" (handsome and proud of their masculinity) has fallen in society, so he takes his revenge by killing her.

1955: Tango was banned because the military took over Argentina, and they believed that people getting together in the middle of the night must be plotting against the government.

Swing dancing was allowed, so young people began to dance Swing, but Tango didn't stop there. Tango continued to be a dance in secret, and it was danced side to side with the American Swing and Rock and Roll.

Juan Carlos Copes, the father of the tango show, was a "show business" man and started to do choreographies even during the ban and sometimes in the next room where all generals were sitting.

Astor Piazzolla, Argentine tango bandoneon player, composer, and arranger whose works revolutionized the traditional tango into a new style, spent some of his youth in Greenwich Village, New York. He studied classical music, and he liked jazz and later, while he studied in Paris, he created an eight instruments (octet) orchestra. On his return to Argentina, he created an orchestra where they played tango with a mix of classical and jazz music. This was called the Tango Nuevo. This is NOT the tango nuevo that everyone knows today.

1980s: When the military dictatorship fell, argentinians brought tango back immediately. Juan Carlos Copes put together a show in Paris where he ironically flew in an argentine military plane and the next day, the "tango argentino" show opened. Since then, excitement and popularity followed in New York the following year.

Tango became more popular because the aristocrats and the upper-class young dancers loved the tango vals (waltz), and it's believed that it was danced a long time ago before this time. A playful walk uses the count of 3, with speed between an english and viennese waltz.

2022: There always will be people who want to follow the tango music and dance authenticity, while others simultaneously will not because they like to incorporate modern twists. Let's hope that Tango continues being danced around the world for ages to come!

In 2009, UNESCO, the United Nations culture organization in International Affairs Office, declared Argentine and Uruguayan Tango to be part of the Intangible Cultural Heritage of Humanity. Unesco Culture goal: "Protecting our heritage and fostering creativity". UNESCO is the only United Nations agency with a mandate in culture for sustainable development.

Present time: Tango today is a "community" that exists independently of other social dance communities. It is a form of professional and amateur musicians, dancers, choreographers, composers, songwriters, teachers of the art, and a national living treasure (a person who possesses to a high degree the knowledge and skills required for performing or re-creating specific elements of the intangible cultural heritage) who embody the Tango culture. Today you can travel around the world from one tango community to the next.

Chapter II

Why Tango and how did I get started?

Why Tango?

Tango is an intense passion, a never-ending romance that keeps you feeling excited, young, and happy.

There are a lot of people that dance to tango without feelings and without understanding the song they are dancing to. Tango could be a song filled with infinite sadness in its lyrics. But some dancers will be laughing and talking, clearly showing they have no understanding of the music they are dancing to. You don't have to know the spanish language to dance the tango. You just need to simply study the dance and music that you love and dance to it every day or every week.

Tango has a dark side with sad lyrics, but also there are a lot of songs about love, passion, and romance. When you understand the music and begin to enjoy dancing with your partner more and more, oftentimes you two can become great friends or even lovers. Many students of mine have either started dating their partner or even gotten married to their partner. That is the magic of tango.

How did I get started?

I started the tango path because of the passion, the control, the intimacy, the dark side, the pain, and the challenge. There are endless reasons for my passion for tango. Tango is not an "I follow your lead" or "you just lead me, and I will follow" type of dance. No, tango is totally different. Both partners need to learn and understand everything equally. It's quite a challenging dance. Not only that, but the philosophy of tango is totally different. It is not like any other form of dance.

Tango is improvisational. Because of this, I find it much more creative than other forms of dance. Remember that improvisation does not mean the same as easy. Quite the contrary! It just makes it limitless. The freedom will make you feel like you want to fly, walk, move, and lead your partner every which way you want. There are no boundaries, no right or wrong. This is one of the many attractions that ultimately led me to tango: its freedom. It allows me, as a leader, to improvise. My passion for the art form motivates me to continue learning.

One of my great teachers Carlos Gavito said, "tango has no nationality. It's a passport, and immigrant's music and dance." Tango has no nationality or specific place where it originates from. It doesn't belong to one person or one community. Anyone can become a great tango dancer if he or she finds a deep passion for it in themselves. After experiencing ballet, contemporary, flamenco, and other latin dances, etc., tango was the winner for me. I carry love and passion in my blood. When I realized my love for it was so deep, I couldn't pull myself away from it. As we like to say, "once you start tango, you will always dance the tango."

Tango has no limit since there is always something new to experience. You will always want to master the new elements you learn. The constant challenge of the dance motivates you to continue practicing. Tango, to me, is my true love. Each song is a three-minute romance with a stranger. Someone you never met before and perhaps might never meet again. But the memory will always remain.

There is no simple word to describe tango. Tango gives me a beautiful sensation that I carry in my heart, in my soul and every time I hear a tango.

-Jon Tariq

I dance tango when I'm sad. I dance tango when I'm happy.

- Jon Tariq

When I dance tango I always worry about only one thing, and that is to be better than I was yesterday.

- Jon Tariq

When I dance tango I forget about the rest of the world.

- Jon Tariq

Remembrance

I once had a moment I will remember for the rest of my life at a Japanese Shinto (Fox) temple where I had the pleasure to do a cheer with sake to their god. While I am looking at the room decorated with white zig zag papers hanging like origami. A prist asked me if I would like hot sake. I answered yes, and he filled up 3 cups of sake, one for me, for him, and one for the god. Then I asked: "Can I ask a question? Where is the god?" I asked the priest.

I will cherish his reply for the rest of my life. He said to me: "There is nothing, but there is something." Tango is like that: for some people, there is nothing, but for others, there is something beyond what one can describe with words. I will never forget that.

I was fortunate enough to learn from Nito Garcia. I remember the times I asked him, "When will I become a better dancer?" He said "Mi hijo, lo tienes" (my son, you have it!). You should never stop learning. If you stop learning, you will go all the way down to zero.

I was fortunate enough to also learn from Carlos Gavito as well. I asked Carlos, "When will I be walking smoothly?" He said, "Count 1,000 steps." And I said, "I did it." Keep counting. Every time, keep counting. I am still counting…

I also learned this from him: the only difference between you and a painter is that the painter will paint a portrait on canvas with his brush, but the dancer's brush is their feet, and their canvas is the dance floor.

My Vals teacher Tete Rusconi said to me in front of everyone in my milonga del barrio, "Tu baila mierda" (you dance like shit). Then, during the performance, and to my surprise, he announced to everyone, "Take Jon's private lessons. He is a great teacher." But I questioned, "Three hours ago, you said I was not good." He said, "I am the only one who can tell you that and no one else."

Chapter III

Jon's Tango Maestro, Professional Friends, and students

Jon's Maestro Nito Garcia and his wife, Elba.

Recently, Nito wrote to Jon and told him what tango means to him:

Tango is the most important thing to ever happen in the artistic world. It is a culture, and it is a learning process by which something arouses the mind, and spirit, and incites the dancer to dance.

Tango is truly argentinian music: it belongs to the city with its flavors, its pains, and its loves. It is not easy to find another art form that is so popular around the world as tango is. It is an artistic manifestation that manifests simultaneously as music, dance, singing, and poetry.

Nito remembers the good old times of tango: where there were more dances than there are now. Back then, it was important for gentlemen to dance with a handkerchief in their hands so the girls wouldn't feel their sweaty hands. And the man always had a suit and tie (and if they didn't, they would rent one at the milonga).

Nito believes that good Maestros are instructors that constantly help students with their learning.

Nito said that he started dancing at 17 by inheritance since he had three uncles who were very good dancers.

One of my uncles lived in my house, and he was the one who took me through tango. He was my teacher in my beginning years.

Nito learned the tango practices that they have between men because, during this time, the mothers would not allow their girls to be seen rehearsing with men. Nito rehearsed three times a week. In ten years, Nito won 15 tango contests, and one of those contests was carried out on television, and the award was for dancing in the most important festival in the skirt province of Cordoba, where Nito came out first. And that was there he met the teacher Osvaldo Pugliese.

When he saw me dance, he contracted me to dance at the Marconi Theater in Buenos Aires in the play Cielo de Barrilete with the dance also in the el dado Rojo confectionery in the Alitalia cantine. And that made us fall in love with Tango and keep it up until today. I'm 87, and I'm still teaching and dancing, full of joy and love.

Carlos Gavito

Carlos Gavito, a prominent figure in the tango world, began his professional dancing career in 1965 in Buenos Aires, Argentina. His distinctive dancing style, characterized by minimalism and pauses, served as inspiration for numerous amateur dancers and professionals. Gavito gained worldwide respect for his didactic approach, emphasizing "less is more" in the art of tango. He performed in the acclaimed show Forever Tango, catapulting him to fame and contributing to the increased interest in learning the intricacies of tango. His influence even extended to my own tango journey as I took classes with him.

A good dancer is one who listens to the music. We dance the music not the steps. Anyone who aspires to dance never thinks about what he is going to do. What he cares about is that he follows the music. You see, we are painters. We paint the music with our feet.

- Carlos Gavito

Omar Vega, a charismatic dancer and teacher, left an indelible mark on the world of tango, milonga, and vals. Known for creating his unique style in milonga, he transcended borders, touring Europe and various U.S. cities. A true gaucho at heart, he brought a folkloric authenticity to his performances. While folkloric dance was part of his upbringing, tango, milonga, and vals became his true passion. Revered as an important teacher of milonga traspie, Vega's legacy lives on through countless students he inspired. He once expressed, "Tango is like a drug: if you don't know how to take it, it'll break you," a sentiment that resonates with his enduring impact on the dance community, immortalizing his contribution to the world of Argentine dance. Personally, I had the honor of learning milonga traspie from him, adding a profound dimension to my appreciation of his artistry.

Facundo Posadas

Facundo Posadas, a Milonguero with roots in the Milonguero tradition, stands out as a notable figure not only in tango but also in Candombe and Milonga con traspié. His journey in the world of tango began in the 1950s, and over the years, Facundo has gained recognition as the foremost Afro-Argentine shaping the tango scene. Beyond his mesmerizing dance skills, he is highly regarded for his influential role as a teacher, and I had the privilege of taking classes with him, adding a personal dimension to my appreciation of his artistry.

The tango is the man and woman in search of each other. It is the search for an embrace, a way to be together, when the man feels that he is a male and the woman feels that she is female, without machismo. She likes to be led; he likes to lead. Disagreements may occur later or they may not. When that moment comes, it is important to have positive and productive dialogue, fifty-fifty. The music arouses and torments, the dance is the coupling of two people defenseless against the world and powerless to change things.

-Juan Carlos Copes

Professional Friends and Students

Guillermina Quiroga

Outstanding dancer, choreographer, and teacher.

She is also an actress with a long list of well-known titles in her curriculum. She integrated the most famous Tango companies in the world, such as

Tango x2, Argentine Tango, and Forever Tango.

Maestra Quiroga tells us her story by answering these questions:

What is Tango to you? Why did you start dancing? Why do you continue to dance?

I grew up surrounded by Tango.

Tango is in our streets, in our everyday life. It is our culture. It's in my roots. I think I was always in contact with tango, but it was not until I saw Tango on TV that I became conscious of the beauty of that particular partner dancing. That is what drove me to find classes to learn, but in 1988, it was not as massive as it is today, where it is easy for people to get access to study tango.

Tango is a very important part of my life; actually, I have a new life thanks to tango: all the people I know around the world, all the places I was able to visit, all the experiences, and the richness of the dancing is contagious and is generously nourishing to the soul.

Tango music makes me connect deep inside with my emotions and gives me the opportunity to open up and express these feelings through my movements and to my partner. It doesn't matter if it is choreography on the stage or I'm improvising with an unknown person at a milonga; together, the music, the embrace, and your partner create the alchemy of tango.

Lifetime Students

Mrs. Emily Lemer and her husband Albert (Alberto)
(his soul rest in peace)

Mr. and Mrs. Lemer had been the best student a teacher can ever have.

Mrs. Lemer is always an enthusiastic learner, committed to doing her best, remains focused, and is always open to new challenges.

When you are Jon's lifetime student, you are part of his family and his family has many benefits. The benefits of dance come in so many forms, he shares his knowledge and experiences and as a teacher, he takes his role very seriously to make judgments about how best to help their students learn. But the most important is that he is a great source of joy, exercise, and artistic expression.

When Maestro Jon Tariq asked Mrs. Lemer what Tango is to her, this is what she said:
THAT IS A HARD ONE! There are so many things to say about Tango. Let's start by saying is movement, lovely music, healthier life of living, and exciting dance.

-Why did you decide to dance the tango?
The steps are beautiful and challenging.

-Why did you decide to take a private tango lesson with Jon?

Because he is sooo good at what he does and understands tango to its roots.

-How much did the tango inspire you and Mr. Lemer?

We loved it.

Alberto introduced me because he loved the music and the passion of the dance. He had done the international tango for years and wanted to try the argentine tango after seeing someone dancing in the subway of New York city.

And the rest is history.

My Dear Friend, Dancer and Event Coordinator

Juan Pablo Vicente

What is tango to him?

Tango is part of my culture, the culture of the city where I was born. Tango is what my grandparents listened to at home, what was playing in the taxis and the bars and coffee shops of Buenos Aires. Tango was on TV, on the streets, and on the radio. Tango is the music where I grew up.

Why did you decide to start to dance, and why tango?
Dancing is something I have always done. I think all humans dance. It is part of our ethos. I started dancing tango after I emigrated to the United States. I was missing something, or perhaps, I found something when I heard tango again after years of being away from Buenos Aires.

And why do you continue to dance?
Like the shark that has to swim to be alive, I can't stop dancing now. Besides, it would be so sad to stop dancing any dance.

LOS CHANTAS

Emilio Teabal on Piano, Sergio Reyes on Violin, David Hadges on Bandoneon, Pablo Lanougere on Double Bass

I'm fortunate to count LOS CHANTAS among my friends. Based in New York City, LOS CHANTAS is a multinational tango ensemble that has been captivating audiences since their inception in 2002. Their repertoire gracefully navigates the diverse landscape of Argentine tango, from the golden era of guardia vieja to the contemporary sounds of today.

With original arrangements featuring songs by legendary artists such as Gardel, Troilo, Salgán, Piazzolla, and others, LOS CHANTAS infuse a fresh and playful spirit into classic tangos. Whether performing in milongas, clubs, theaters, or various venues around New York, their music adds a unique and vibrant touch to the city's cultural scene. I'm always thrilled to support and enjoy the incredible talent that LOS CHANTAS brings to the world of tango!

Not only are LOS CHANTAS incredibly talented musicians, but as my friends they join many of my celebrations where they bring a lively and unforgettable atmosphere to the festivities.

Hector Del Curto

Fortunate to call him a friend, Hector Del Curto is a Grammy-winning musician, composer, recording artist, and educator hailed by the New York Times as a 'splendid player' and recognized as one of the world's most sought-after bandoneonists. Born in Buenos Aires, Hector's musical journey began early, winning the title of 'Best Bandoneon Player Under 25' in Argentina at the age of 17. His remarkable talent led him to join the orchestra of the legendary Osvaldo Pugliese, the 'Last Giant of Tango.'

In 1998, Hector became the music director of Forever Tango, a Broadway hit that continues to tour globally.

He founded the Eternal Tango Orchestra, a ten-piece ensemble debuting at New York's Lincoln Center, and the Hector Del Curto Tango Quintet. As a Grammy-winning artist, his self-produced albums, 'Eternal Piazzolla' and 'Eternal Tango,' have gained international acclaim, featured by BBC News and Public Radio International.

Hector's perspective on tango is profound, seeing it as the expression of Buenos Aires'. diverse culture, shaped by immigrants from around the world. Tango, for him, is identity, a cultural journey reflecting his family's roots in countries like France, Spain, Italy, Ukraine, Poland, and Germany.

Music, a vital part of personal development, has been integral to Hector's life. Encouraged by his family, he started with the guitar but found his true voice in the bandoneon, a familial instrument. Since then, the bandoneon has been Hector's means of self-expression, shaping his remarkable musical career.

Chapter IV

Tango Etiquette and Superstitions

Preparation for the Milonga

- Proper hygiene is a must. You will be dancing with many people for many hours. It is important that you shower before getting dressed and put on some deodorant. If you have bad breath, have some mints on hand. If you sweat a lot, bring other shirts to change into. If your hands get sweaty, use a handkerchief.
- For the ladies, do not wear any creams, oils, or liquid stockings that might stain the men's trousers and jackets. Keep your perfumes soft and light. Less is more.
- Always dress to impress.

- If you attend the Milonga with a partner or a significant other, the first and last dance is for your partner or significant other.
- "Cabeceo" (head not): an eye invitation where a man or woman raises his eyebrows to make a signal to a woman, asking her if she wants to dance. If she accepts, she will smile; but if she does not, she will look away.
- Tanda: a tango music set that is played in either three or four groups. The dancing couple should expect to dance to three to four songs with the same person.
- Cortinas: are the intermission of a tango song; they are between tandas. They're played for about 30 seconds.

- Couples should circulate the dance floor counterclockwise.
- Always take it one tanda at a time. If you enjoyed dancing with someone and would like the chance to dance again with that person, you can always say something like, "I hope we can dance again."
- Never thank the dance partner after the first or second dance, but instead, always wait until you are done with the tanda. Otherwise, they are going to think you want them to get lost. When the ladies say, "thank you," the gentlemen always respond with, "it was my pleasure."
- Always finish the dance (tanda) before you leave the person.
- Gentlemen should always escort the woman back off the dance floor, when possible, to her chair or to the end of the dance floor.
- Never teach/instruct anyone on the dance floor.

- Never use excuses on the dance floor about how bad you are or that you made a mistake. Just enjoy the moment.
- Never criticize anyone on the dance floor.
- Tango is done in silence because you are speaking with your body.
- During the cortina, visually find your next dance partner.
- Never cross the dance floor during a tanda or during a performance. Wait for the cortina.
- In some places, they have set codes: Never change your shoes at the table or in the room. Use the common area or the restroom.
- No matter how good you are at tango, you should always dance according to your partner's ability.
- A Milonga is not a competition of who dances better or who can do the most embellishments. It is just about enjoying the dance.
- Always welcome, encourage, and dance with beginners.

- The Birthday Celebration: The birthday person goes to the center of the room, and the opposite sex dancers will line up or make a circle around them. Every single dancer will then dance with the birthday girl or boy. Please keep in mind that this is different from National Tango Day, celebrated on December 11 in Argentina, which commemorates the birthdays of legendary singer Carlos Gardel and orchestra conductor Julio de Caro. This night is celebrated with a spectacular dance exhibition in Corrientes, a city in northeastern Argentina.

Superstition

- Never dance to Carlos Gardel's song "Adios Muchachos" because it is believed to be the song he sang right before his death. It is very bad luck to play and/or dance to this song.
- In Argentina, they do not play Carlos di Sarli as a first tanda in the Milongas. It's believed to bring back luck.

- There is a superstition about Pugliese that he brings good luck. Some people even call him Saint Pugliese (Santo Pugliese). In one major event in Argentina, with some technical issues affecting the event, someone put on a Pugliese CD, and all the technical issues went away. Because of this event, it is said that Pugliese brings good luck.

Good Luck!

Chapter V

Types and Styles of Tango

The frame: close embrace vs. open embrace (abrazo or "embrace")

A close embrace is the silent, intimate, courageous communication channel between the leader and the follower. This connection can only exist between them because their upper torsos are against each other, able to feel the other's heartbeat.

The Tango's frame is flexibly adjusting to different steps and may vary from being quite close to open to a "V" frame which is not very comfortable because the girl has to walk sideways.

Tango Apilado is a style of tango dancing where couples lean forward against each other, with contact maintained at the level of the chest, and it is only done during a close embrace. It is important to remember that each partner never relies on the other for balance, neither during an open nor close embrace. But it is also fine if the follower gives 5% to 10% weight to their partner.

An open embrace is when the dancers are at arm's length, and their hands are their only contact.

Variations in the tango open and close Embrace

Tango was always danced and performed in close and open embrace.

I like to combine the elements: lifts, jumps, close embrace, and open embrace. This way, you can bring excitement and satisfaction to everybody sitting and watching your show.

Milonguero style tango is typically danced with a slightly leaning posture that typically joins the torsos of the two dancers (in an embrace called apilado) to create a merge that still allows a little bit of distance between the couple's feet.

The couple never loosens their embrace. This embrace typically involves the woman's left shoulder as close to her partner's right shoulder as her left shoulder is to his right. The woman's left arm is often draped behind the man's neck, which I find to be the wrong way to dance.

Our hand should sit on the shoulder of the partner. This positioning gives freedom to the leaders and the followers and ensures no one feels choked. Sometimes the followers can look like they are in their leaders' frame, which doesn't look good.

The Milongero embrace: It is said by some practitioners that Milongueros just want to dance, even if it's just 15-20 steps.

Orillero-style: This style is an older style of tango whose name suggests that it may have had its origins in the streets of the poor area of Buenos Aires. Later on, it came to refer to the man dancing around the edge of the woman. In either case, Orillero-style tango was not considered acceptable in the refined salons of central Buenos Aires. This style developed around the 1919's.

Tango Escenario (stage tango)

This type of tango is danced on stage (show tango). This style is originally from Villa Urquiza, and the term 'Estilo Villa Urquiza' has been used to identify a style of tango that was popular in the barrio of Villa Urquiza during the 1940s. Tango Escenario is danced in both open and close embrace with exaggerated movements often taken from ballet and acrobatics. A great example of this style was Antonio Todaro, the most creative and renovator ever on stage, and fantasia tango and a great teacher. Celia Blanco is another example of a great teacher and dancer.

Fantasia (show tango)

The term "tango fantasia" refers to an exhibition style of dancing from the Villa Urquiza style of tango but uses embellishments more extensively and adds dramatic poses, ganchos, and high boleos.

This style was developed for use in exhibitions during breaks in milongas but was eventually brought to the stage. As the stage style evolved, some people distinguished the result as tango escenario (exhibition tango as fantasia). Today we use a combination of traditional tango moves and show performance movements to create a good routine for the exhibition.

Milonga: is a dance you dance with Milonga music. It incorporates the same basic elements as Argentine Tango but with faster rhythmic moves and without pauses.

A Milonga is also a social event or location for tango dancing, or in other words, a tango dance party. People who dance at milongas are known as milongueros.

Milonga lisa: (classic milonga or milonga de salon) Dancers move and step to every beat or skip one beat of the music.

Milonga con traspie: (tripping) In this advanced version of the milonga, dancers may take double steps or incorporate moves that involve four steps.

Tango de salon: We dance every day as a social dance at the milongas and as a salon exhibition too.

Traditional tango de salon requires that dancers respect the line of dance. The embraces and movements can also vary considerably across individual styles. This is a tango style where dancers need to connect the torso and give little space in the lower frame.

Club-style Tango: May have developed as Orillero-style dance and then moved indoors and later adapted their rhythmic dance to smaller spaces. Club-style tango is typically danced to the ric-tic-tic rhythm that is prominent in the music of Juan D'Arienzo and Rodolfo Biagi.

Vals, Vals Criollo, Valsito or Vals Cruzado, or tango waltz (named for its orchestration-instrumentation): All these names mean the same thing, Waltz.

argentine vals, the name derives from the germans waltz, referring to the particular dance performed by couples with rotating and gliding movements.

It is a slow three-beat measure (slow, quick-quick), elegantly turning couples several times on the spot. It is danced playfully with speed varying between the english waltz and the viennese waltz.

This dance was brought to argentina by austrian and german immigrants. This dance conquered the most exquisite dance halls worldwide and continues to do so.

Alternative or Nuevo tango – Music, dance, and the social behaviors are different. It is danced in an open, elastic, or loose embrace with a very upright posture and a great emphasis on the dancers maintaining their own axes. This style might be considered a show version style because of the showy elements that are not appropriate for dancing in crowded venues. This style started to pop up around the world in the 1990s. It was danced to different music types and included new combinations and step patterns like ochos, cadenas, linear boleos, volcadas, and single spins. Tango Nuevo is often danced by the younger generations of tango dancers, and 21st-century musicians are creating special music for it. When the new tango came out, some people started teaching and performing it. Because of this, we now have Nuevo Tango teachers who teach and perform this style exclusively. New trends that can be found in this style include floppy pants, open red or white shoes, and dancing with no embrace.

Tango Queer: a tango without distinction or regard for sex or sexual traditional heteronormative orientation and roles. When dancing, they often exchange the leader and follower roles.

In the first years of tango, argentina was mostly populated by male working-class imigrants. In fact, one statistic claims there was a consistent surplus of argentine women over argentine men.

According to the World Bank collection of development indicators, there were seven men to every woman in the country for marriage or companionship.

The men were dancing with one another to brush up on moves before a potential female suitor came along. There were plenty of photos that showed a man dancing with a man. The first one was published in 1903 in the magazine Caras y Caretas.

1940-1950: Same-sex dancers were banned from Tango clubs - Milongas because it signifies tendencies.

In 2001, the world's first official Queer Milonga opened in Hamburg, Germany and argentina's inaugural International Queer Tango Festival opened the same year. These two simultaneous events marked the beginning of the Queer Tango movement.

Canyengue: is a historical form of tango from the 1920s and early 1930s. Since practitioners cannot guarantee historical accuracy, the dance may or may not be accurately captured by its current dancers because they acquire their own interpretation of the dance.

The dance is done with a V embrace, exaggerated short steps, and bended knees, and the woman never executes a cross. The music has a fast rhythm characterized by a ric-tic and double-time rhythms typical of Milonguero-style. At the time, women wore long, tight dresses.

Candombe: roots came originally from the Brazilian dance called Canyengue. It is a folk dance performed at carnival, mainly by brazilian and uruguayans of african ancestry. Some people adapted their music to dance to milonga dance, and they call it the tango negro or milonga candombe. Ex: *Tango Negro by Juan Carlos Caceres or Milonga Sentimental-Jorge Valdez*

Liquid tango: this is a dance with both an open and close embrace that allows you to incorporate different styles of tango simultaneously, especially Nuevo tango. This is not yet a style of dancing. It is just another way.

Which style is authentic?

These styles have some degree of authenticity because they pull from the practices and historical guides of argentine tango as it is and was danced in Buenos Aires and other cities in Argentina.

Some styles are more popular in a particular city and should not be confused with authenticity since it may result from different styles serving different social purposes during a specific time. For example, Fantasia and Tango Escenario are authentic for exhibition dancing but not social dancing.

Dancers don't need wings to fly.

- Jon Tariq

A dancer should stay inspired with their dance goals.

- Jon Tariq

Chapter VI

Tango music

A Brief History...

Tango music was once viewed as the most popular music genre. Its distinctive music style has made it a worldwide music sensation. Tango music is characterized by a build of a predictable, repetitive musical rondo where the main theme is interrupted by interludes and repeated throughout the song, sometimes with a different rhythm or melody.

Tango music can be instrumental, or it can feature a vocalist. From 1900-1917, the most typical instruments, in the beginning, were the trios: guitar (including the 7, 9 or 11 strings), violin and flute.

The quartets: guitar, violin, flute, and added the bandoneon (also known as the "tango accordion" in the

US). 1917 the guitar was replaced by the piano. 1925 The sextet started with 2 violins, 2 bandoneons, piano, and double bass. The formation of the "orquesta típica" (orchestra)A tango orchestra, known in Spanish as a, tends to feature the following instruments: 4 bandoneons, 4 violins, piano, double bass, and vocals.

The Tango Rhythm

Every piece of music has a basic beat, like a heart beating, a clock ticking, or the sound of footsteps. This beat may be fast, slow, or in between. The speed of the beat is called the tempo. The tempo is set by the musicians, and the dancers will match their movements to the tempo accordingly.

Marcato and Syncopation

The two main rhythms in tango are Marcato and Sincopa.

Marcato Beats (4 beats)

Marcato: This is a march beat that has four quarter notes in Staccato (music composed of tones that are short and non-continuous) way and with strong accents in the 1 and 3 and the weak accents in the 2 and 4. It was very popular in the 1920s.

The first note is played a little louder than the rest (for example, val's (waltz) music is ONE-two-three-ONE-two-three ONE-two-three). When four quarter notes are put into a measure, the musician usually plays the first and third notes the loudest. Almost every dance has a set rhythm that matches the measures of the music.

Syncopation

Those are the ones who fall in unexpected places.

Some advanced rhythm dancers are so good at stepping exactly on the beat that they like to add diversity by going off the beat. This is called syncopation. These dancers would do something even harder: they will begin with step patterns on other beats than the first beat of a measure and work with step patterns that fit exactly within the metric structure of the music.

Tango dancers do something even more amazing; they will improvise step patterns and rhythms as they dance. In a minute of dancing at the average tempo of tango music, this could mean unlimited steps or any combination in between! It could also mean some slow steps that are even slower than others and times in which the dancers stop moving altogether.

3-3-2 Music example:

Arrabal – Pedro Laurenz (1937)

Astor Piazzolla- Libertango (Tango Nuevo 1974)

Balada Para Un Loco by Osvaldo Pugliese (1970)

Comme Il Faut and Toda Mi Vida by Anibal Troilo (1938)

Che Tango Che, Escualo, Jacinto Chiclana, Verano Porteño by Astor Piazzolla

Mala Junta 1943 by Osvaldo Pugliese

Negracha - Pugliese (1948)

Nonino and Zum by Color Tango

Orlando Goni – Alfredo Gobbi (1949)

Tierra Querida – Pugliese (1944)

Ric-Tic-Tic is not a rhythm but an ormentation within the marcato high register.

Ric-tic-tic is onomatopoeia (a word that sounds like the noise it describes) for the *staccato rhythms* (articulation, short rhythm (cortito), detached and spiky rhythm) of this music as one, two; ric, tic, tic; one, two; ric, tic, tic.

The characteristic rhythm of this music is actually created through a variation in accented beats and yields an alternation of single-time and double-time rhythms. For example, the music might be played one and two and one and two and dancers will say slow, slow; quick, quick, slow; slow, slow movements, which are prominent in the music of Juan D'Arienzo, Rodolfo Biagi, and other golden-era tango orchestras.

What makes a tango a tango?

A typical tango consists of five sections. Each section consists of four phrases (represent lyrics in a song). Each phrase consists of four measures. Each measure (in 4/4 time) consists of four beats (two "strong" downbeats and two "weak" beats). The tempo of instrumental tango is 120-132 BPM, and for singers 110 to 120BPM. Tempo has a lot to do with the tango style of dancing. The Sincopa gives tango its drama. Tango music often ends with a "chan-chan" sound. The main chords used when the music is in the minor key are the chords i, V, V, i In A minor, these chords would be Am, E7 E7 Am

What is Tango Musicality

Musicality is the dancer's ability to become one with the music for the dancer to hear, interpret, and move to the music.

Today Tango dancers are spending time learning about the music they are dancing to. The dancers that understand this concept quickly become better dancers. The music provides harmony between the dancer, dance partner, and everyone with whom they share the floor.

Tango Dance Groups and Orchestras

The first organized "group" of tango musicians started in Buenos Aires between 1870-1890s by three afro-argentines: violinist casimiro alcorta, clarinet player known as Sinforoso, and piano player Rosendo Mendizabal.

Francisco Canaro (1888-1964) was an uruguayan violinist and tango orchestra leader from the generation prior to tango's "Big Four." His recordings, both traditional tango and Milongas, are noted as beautiful and melodic Ex: in 1912, he composed "Pinta Brava" ("Fierce Look").

Popular- tangos before 1900

-Andate a la recoleta (1880)

Dame la lata by Juan Perez – (1880) ("Gimme the tinplate").

This particular song talks about the life of prostitutes, pimps, and brothel managers and how Tinplates or metal tokens (this was their money and how it changed hands) were used in the prostitution scene in Buenos Aires at the time the song was written. The Brothel managers receive the cash from clients while the prostitutes hand them to their pimps.

-El queco by Lino Galeano (Approx. 1874)

-El Talar by Prudencio Aragon (1900-1930)

-Que si que no Y a mí qué Eloísa D'Herbil (1900-1930)

"Guardia Vieja" style (old guard) For example, "Sabado" from 1930. This style characterized by an orchestra of six with very little power musicians. The dancer will normally dance to this style with small, simple steps in a close embrace.

Accentuated dynamic rhythm: "Retirao" (1939)

Salon style

The king of the Guardia Vieja Salon style was Roberto Firpo. He was recognized as one of the most recognized composers of the time and for having the best technical equipment at the time. In the beginning, when the piano was introduced. It was an overwhelming sound that would draw out the other instruments. Firpo managed to combine all to sound good in the orquesta tipica in, which was the only orchestra that was recording at the time. Firpo was also a great pensioned cultivator of the waltz Ex: "Noche Calvorosa" and "Palida Sombra" Ex: De salon style- "Re Fa Si" 1916-1918.

Refasi by Juan D'Arienzo 1935 was a nice version of the same song.

1940-1950 - was when orchestras brought singers in, such as Roberto Rufino, Francisco Fiorentino and Alberto Marino. The dancers wanted to dance slowly to a more precise beat to match the beat and express the feelings of the lyrics. Ex: "Tristeza Marina" (1943)

After 1959, the sound of tango music changed with the invention of the stereophonic. To use the new modern sound, the dancers wanted to be elegant and sophisticated, so they made the embrace more flexible and added many more poses. It is a great example of an elegant, sophisticated tango. "Re fa si" 1959 Osvaldo Fresedo first one on stereo.

Juan D'Arienzo y su Orquesta Típica was known as "El Rey del Compas" ("King of the Beat"). Between 1930-1970, he made and recorded about 1,000 tangos. He made even the most reluctant dancer stand up and dance to his rhythm and beat. In 1935, D'Arienzo imposed his style of four beats exclusively, like the tick-tick of a watch, which made dancers focus on enjoying his rhythms. He put accents in the tempos (beats), which are played Marcato (with emphasis), added solo violins in the middle of songs, and periods of silence in order to give the dancer an opportunity to be creative and dramatic with their moves. He also added variations (a formal technique where the material is repeated in an altered form) near the end of his songs that no other orchestra did and pizzicato (when an instrument is plucked with the fingers instead of a bow). Ex: "Vaca" & "Loca" & "Enamorado".

Juan D'Arienzo was a very exciting man. He added Variations with five bandoneons playing together which allows dancers to be dynamic, make changes, accelerates, and express many different feelings in the same piece. Also, the four strong beat pieces allow the dancer to dance with sharper moves and faster walks. Closer to the end, he liked to add a violin solo which allowed the dancers to be more creative. I see why he got the title of King of the beat!

*"**Young people like me**. They like my tangos because they are rhythmic, nervous up-tempos. Youth are after that: happiness, movement. If you play for them a melodic tango and out of beat, they won't like it," said D'Arienzo.*

Four Strong Beats:

"Tango Don Juan" (1937)

"Derecho Viejo" (1939)

"La Clavada" (1940)

Violin Solos:

"Que Noche" (1937)

"Loca" (1946)

Variations:

"El Choclo" (1937)

"Paciencia" (1937)

Sincopas:

"El Puntazo" (1951)

"No mientas" (1938)

Carlos di Sarli was known around the world as "El Señor del Tango" ("The Gentleman of Tango"). It is said that he made one of the most elegant and melodic orchestras. His orchestras went through different musical style changes from 1926-1950. This musical evolution also affected the way dancers danced to his music. Ex: "Junto a tu Corazon" (1942)

Anibal Troilo (1914–1975), also known as "El Gordo" ("The Fat") or "Pichuco" (nickname), played the bandoneon with so much excitement that he became the most admired and expressive bandoneon player. His instrumental music was to hear dance and could be an instrument or not, which emphasizes a combination of melody and rhythm with lots of bandoneon solos on the left hand of this instrument.

He recorded with Francisco Fiorentino from 1937 to 1943.

Ex: "Con Toda La Voz Que Tengo" (1941)

"Malena (1942)

"Total pa que sirvo" (1941)

"Tristezas de la calle Corrientes" (1942)

Osvaldo Pugliese (1905-1995) created a new style of tango music that was dramatic and with long pauses. His music was considered the most beautiful, passionate, and intense music that tango has ever known. He accentuated the 1st to 3rd beats. They call the rhythm Yumba. Ex: La Yumba 1946, Malandraca 1949 Negracha 1948

Sebastián Piana, Argentine Pianist, leader, and composer, reintroduced the Milonga rhythm with "Milonga Sentimental" in 1936.

Measuring pitch

Before 16th century there was no way to measure pitch (pitch, or frequency, is cycles per second in a very short time interval) because there was no way of measuring time with enough accuracy. Even up until the 18th century, there was no standard pitch from country to country, but from region to region and village to village, the "standard" pitch was the village church organ. Because it was hard to re-tune, it was easier to have everyone tune to the organ.

Mozart's piano builder (Johann Andreas Stein) worked at 421.6Hz. If we play baroque music on period instruments today, tune to 415Hz, the pitch was different at the time. Bandoneons were manufactured at a pitch of 435Hz, and tango orchestras played at that pitch. The bandoneon is not an instrument you want to re-tune before a gig because it cannot be tuned by the player, but only by a specialist.

Alexander's gift

The Congress of Vienna (1814-1815) became the center of the world because they were created to re-organize

Europe after the Napoleonic Wars. This was a very lavish event where all major powers sent their most important statesman, and Tsar Alexander of Russia attended himself.

Alexander presented the Austrian Army with a gift, a new set of musical instruments tuned to 440Hz, a lot higher than what they were used to. Then the world slowly converted to a standard pitch of 440Hz. Tango orchestras were the exception because of their use of bandoneons.

In May 1939, an international conference in London recommended changing the standardized tuning of 440Hz for bandoneons. Some bandoneon manufacturers continued at 435Hz. The tango orchestras themselves had already decided to retune.

Analysis of the D'Arienzo transfers of CTA by Frank Jin, has found that the D'Arienzo orchestra recorded its last session at 435Hz on March 3rd, 1939. The next session on April 18th was recorded at 440Hz. These dates would be consistent with the orchestra recording one session immediately after the carnival. From this moment on, the instrument importers retuned the instruments from 435Hz to 440Hz, but the outbreak of World War II brought an end to the export of musical instruments by the end of 1941.

Tango's evolution

Carlos Gardel popularized Tango like no one before, but his death emphasized big tango bands more than individual singers in this era. Tango singers wanted to sing with guitar accompaniment because Gardel was the engine that started the guitar group's accompaniment aside Corsini and Magaldi. So the singers dream of singing with a guitar.

In the 1950s, rock-n-roll took over the airways, which gave tango a new form, and Astor Piazzolla's music took the forefront with his compositions with a complex harmonic and contrapuntal music technique.

The musical style of Tango Nuevo broke the traditional tango rules and incorporated many jazz influences, complex harmonies, and elaborate arrangements.

Some of the most notable composers of Tango Nuevo style music were Astro Piazzola, and Eduardo Rovira.

Today's Tango or Tango Fusion includes
Pabo Aslan, Agustin Guerrero, Julian Graciano, Juan Pablo Navarro and Diego Schissi, to name a few.

NeoTango or electro tango: is a new sound that is very appealing to 21st-century audiences where tango music incorporates electronic influences such as electronic instruments and computer-edited vocals. Luciano Superville ex: Gotan Proyect , Otros Aires and Bajo fondo.

New Tango Songs

Tango changed once again, which borrowed the orchestra-based influences of early tango history and mixed it with a contemporary themed lyrical style. The most notable performers and bands of this new type of tango music are Julian Peralta, Orquesta Rascacielos, Altertango, Ciudad Baigón, Victoria di Raimondo and Pacha González.

Tango playlist:

"9 De Julio" by Juan D'Arienzo (1935)

"Al Compas de un Tango" by Lucio Demare

"El choclo," "El Pimpolla," "La Vida del Carretero" and

"El Negro Alegre" by Ángel Villoldo (1903-1907)

"El entrerriano" by Rosendo Mendizabal (1896)

"El Taita" by Higinio Cazón (1905)

"El Tango Patagones" by Gabino Ezeiza (1905)

"Infiltrado" by Bajofondo

"Jamás Retornarás" by Miguel Calo

"La Canguela" (1889)

"La Puñalada" by Juan D'Arienzo (1937)

"Mano a mano" by Hugo del Carril (1923)

"Milonga Sentimental" by Sebastián Piana

"Pobre Flor" by Alfredo De Angelis

"Por Una Cabeza" by Itzhak Perlman

"Vida Mia" by Osvaldo Fresedo

"Chique" by Juan D'Arienzo

"Emancipacion – Orquesta" by Osvaldo Pugliese (1955)

Ángel D'Agostino

Carlos Di Sarli

Francisco Lomuto

Hugo del Carril

Juan Carlos Howard

Juan D'Arienzo

Lucio Demare

Osvaldo Fresedo

Osvaldo Pugliese

List of tango bandleaders during the Golden Age of tango: 1937-1955

Adolfo Carabelli

Alberto Di Paulo

Alfredo De Angelis

Alfredo Gobbi

Angel D'Agostino

Aníbal Troilo

Armando Cupo

Carlos di Sarli

Ciriaco Ortiz

Domingo Federico

Donato Racciatti

Edgardo Donato

Enrique Mario Francini

Enrique Rodriguez

Florindo Sassone

Francisco Canaro

Francisco Lomuto

Francisco Rotundo

Héctor Varela

Horacio Salgán

José Basso

Jose Garcia Y Sus Zorros Grices

Juan Cambareri

Juan d'Arienzo

Juan Polito

Lucio Demare

Manuel Buzón

Miguel Caló

Osmar Maderna

Osvaldo Pugliese

Ricardo Malerba

Ricardo Tanturi

Rodolfo Biagi

Traditional and contemporary Tango music and Jazz

Hector Del Curto: Following a relocation to New York, he found himself impelled to create an orquesta tipica, leading to the birth of the Eternal Tango Orchestra. This venture not only reflected his passion for the genre but also showcased his commitment to preserving and innovating within the rich traditions of tango.

Los Chantas are a multinational tango ensemble based in New York City. Their repertoire draws from the great Argentine tango tradition from the guardia vieja to the present.

Traditional and contemporary Tango music

Julian Graciano-Argentine Guitarist, composer and Tango researcher.

Author of the "Real Book of Tango" Editorial Melos / Ricordi Argetina. A collection of more than 700 works divided into 6 volumes.

Composer, producer and director of his projects Tango in Tres and Graciano 4 quartet.

Transcriptions from solo instruments to orchestras. Arrangements for orchestras, adaptations and piano reductions.

Teacher of the National Academy of Tango

Julian Graciano is the one who has review my music information here in my book and I will always be grateful.

Jon's Favorite Tango Mastro's

Osvaldo Pugliese, Roberto Goyeneche, Ricardo Tanituri Campos, Miguel Calo, Carlos Di Sarli, Angle D' Agostino, Edgardo Donato, Angel Vargas, Alberto Castillo, Enrique Rodiguez, Hector Verela, Osvaldo Fresedo, Juan D' Arienzo, Rodaolfo Biagii, Anibal Trilo, Alfredo De Angelis, Romantica Milongera, Astro Piazzola and Hector Del Curto

Jon's Favorite Playlist

"Esta noche en Buenos Aires" Angel Vargas

"Angelica" , "Illusion Azul" Alfredo Angelis (vals)

"Buscandote" Osvaldo Fresedo

"Café Dominguez " and "Tres Esquina" "Tango de los Ángeles" Ángel D'Agostino

"Cantemos Corazon" "Junto a Ti Corazon" "Tormento" "Fumando Te Espero" Carlos Disarli

"Corazon de Oro" "Poema" "Reliquias Portenas"

"El Adio's" Edgardo Donato

"El Compass de los Corazones" "Que te importa" Miguel Calo'

"Esta Tarde Gris" Anibal Triolo

"Flor de Monserrat" Rodolfo Biagi

"Hasta Siempre Amor" Jorge Valdez

"Historia de Amor" "Que Tarde has Venido"

"Mi Dolor" Juan D'Arienzo

"Nada mas" "Paciencia" "Espuela" "Milonga la

Cicatriz" "Milonga del Corazon" "Milonga Vieja

Milonga" "Milonga de mis Amores",

"Oblivion" Astro Piazzola

"Oigo tu Voz" Tanturi Compas

"Que falta que me hace" Miguel Calo'

"Recuerdos" Castillo Alberto

"Remembranzas", "A Evaristo Carriego", Forever Tango

“Recuerdo” “Zum” “Pata Ancha” OswaldoPlugliese

“Sur” Goyeneche

“Tango Negro”, “Vuelvo al Sur”, “Darsena” Carlos Caceres

“A Mis Viejos” Anibal Troilo

“Michelangelo, Escualo, Verano Porteño, La Muerte del Angel” Astor Piazzolla

“Milonga de Buenos Aires” Francisco Canaro

“Nostalgias” Juan Carlos Cobian

“Milonga”, “Milonga solitaire portena”, “Tango Mandira”, “No mientas”, “ensalo bien” Juan D’Arienzo

Remember, let the music do something to you and get emotional.

- Jon Tariq

When you hug your partner, remember only two things, the music and the connection.

- Jon Tariq

Chapter VII

What Makes a Tango Dancer a Good Dancer?

Dance is the movement of the body in a rhythmic way to express an idea or an emotion, release energy, or just simply have fun as a hobby or as part of your profession. The only key to being a good dancer is *wanting* to be a good dancer.

Dance improves muscular strength, muscle tone, endurance, motor fitness, increased aerobic fitness, and weight management.

The dancer's responsibilities include showing up on time for rehearsals, performances, and Milongas dance social) and dress fittings, practicing routines, and keeping fit. All these are important to keep up with the skills.

How to dance Tango

First thing first:

The man: Must hold themselves the proper way to move and look gracefully.

The woman: Must also hold herself the proper way by staying tall and steady but flexible.

Being Tango dancers, we don't move even one step without music.

Tango is about feelings.

- Jon Tariq

Argentine Tango dance starts from you, then your partner, and then the music.

- Jon Tariq

Tango is characterized by dancing counterclockwise in the line of dance around the dance floor while walking outside (cross system) and inside (parallel system) the follower.

Always remember that Tango is an improvisation dance with much more open ideas to lead and follow the right way. This is teamwork. Both need to know their portion to move properly in the right way with the flow among other dancers at the Milongas.

It's important when a man invites a woman to dance, to use the head gesture "Cabeceo". A woman also could ask her dance partner, her teachers and Tango Friends. No obligation to ask a stranger, too, but don't get offended if you get turned down by that stranger.

If you accept the request of the partner by signaling him back from across the floor, it means you're accepting his request to dance a Tanda with him.

Stand up and allow the leader to reach out to you. The proper etiquette at this time is that the man should always go toward the dance partner; nothing is wrong if the girls want to meet him too.

When in front of each other, the leader raises his left arm and the follower raises the right arm, holds hands and then they connect. The leader will wrap his right arm around the follower's frame (waist or mid-back), the follower places the left arm on the leader's shoulder. Now they are embracing.

The followers always follow the leader's torso

for a better connection, the shoulder should be maintained evenly straight, and hips, knees, and toes must be facing your partner during the walks (Caminar). The dancers must follow the music, and they dance their tango steps and combinations to the beat, expressing their feelings in their own unique way.

Tango dancers will spend the majority of practice time refining their moves.

Women should slightly lean forward to create the tent position (Carpa) to give 5 to 10% weight and to take off the weight of their heels.

There are always two ways to dance stand straight or slightly lean.

Also, remember that the lower frame carries the upper frame or your legs carry the body. Don't push your upper frame first let the legs flow first and then follow the upper body.

As a beginner, you have two frames. This idea makes it easy for the new dancers to understand the concept in a simple manner.

Advance dancers divide their frames into more than two frames, plus they have the right and left sides.

The leader should not start walking without connecting properly with his partner. They should always give an extra split-second to the followers in case they want to do embellishments.

When you are at the Milonga, remember that you are not at the park or at the gym. You should follow the Milonga code of Etiquette (Códigos).

The difference between cross and parallel system

When we go to the Salida, the leader walks outside of the follower frame with the right leg, and the follower walks back with the left leg. The followers will go to the cross on 4 counts, which is considered a cross system.

The follower's "back-walks" is extremely important in Tango. The followers walk backward 90% of their dance, projecting and transferring their weight from one side to the next, back and forth, keeping the weight on their ball of the foot to maintain balance.

Avoid bouncing up and down. Don't bend your knees, and don't lock your knees.

There is a fluidity in the steps when done correctly. That comes with practicing the walks over and over again.

The followers will never hang on to their leader.

The Ochos are as important moves as every other step in tango because they open the door to many Figures, for example Sacadas or Lapiz or many more steps: Ochos or Caminar (walks) have the same logic and the direction is 45° rotation either forward or back.

A dancer's good posture is when all the weight is in the ball of the foot. Dance in the center. Elbows in front of the body. This structure is never broken down. When you dance, all the upper frame will move all together: shoulder, elbow, and chest. Keep the structure. That's the reason I always tell my students to dance for themselves first, then for their partner, and then with the music. This way, they learn to balance and carry themselves gracefully.

A dancer should always think that everyone is watching them. Only this feeling brings you to the next level and makes you self-aware enough to care when and how you move and take your steps. Just like the song "Pensalo bien" says, think well before you take a step. If you take a wrong step, you can't take it back.

When done properly, dancing tango feels like two souls moving around the dance floor. It is like feeling thirsty and then seeing a whole river before you. A good Tango dance can leave you feeling speechless and satisfied.

The Tango walk

The Tango walk is the fundamental step or movement of the tango. This is a game of the entire body. Toe, knees, legs, hips, core, torso, holding a good posture, shoulders, to connect and embrace and then bring whatever feelings you have to walk with a perfect balance, grace, and it emphasizes femininity or masculinity for the man.

We call it the parallel system of walking:

-Feet are always touching the ground

-The ankles and thighs always rub against each other

-Maintain constant bending at the knees (only one leg always has the weight).

Start the walk:

-The center is the center of our body

-The torso slightly tilted forward

-Shoulders are parallel with hips

-Torso and hips move together (Only in the walk but not in the turns. In turns, the hips first and then the torso)

-Keep the weight on the hips and on the ball of the foot.

-Relax the knee so that the other one passes. You always have to have the same level (no going up and down with your knees).

Weight Shifting

Don't transfer your weight without the leader's lead.

If the leader is not shifting your weight, don't do it. This is especially important for beginners to understand how important weight shifting is in Argentinian tango.

The leader will transfer your weight at any moment, so you should always be in the weight-shifting process.

Remember, you're not standing for the bus or train. Also, you're not standing like a Western cowboy waiting to dual. You are dancing the tango, and it's important to understand your body, your frame, and the weight-shifting concept to make it easy for the leaders and followers to dance the proper way.

In this book, you will find a chart that will teach you the proper way to weight shift. Learn it, but always remember you are dancing on a dance floor, not in the street. Appreciate the beauty and put some effort into understanding your frame and your partners' frame and the position of the weight shifting or shifted or collected.

There are so many great teachers worldwide. If you still don't understand the concept, you must discuss and practice with a teacher. Take a private lesson so the teacher can explain the idea of weight shifting properly.

It's important to look graceful, executing every move or projecting every step. It is a careful process you can't learn by watching movies or reading books.

Some people think they can improve without even taking dance lessons. You are wrong.

- Jon Tariq

One of the fastest ways to improve your dancing is simply to have a goal to work towards.

- Jon Tariq

Discipline and practice will give you the skill you need to tango, and there really is no way around it.

- Jon Tariq

Stop wanting things and start participating in the process of creating them.

- Jon Tariq

Some people seem to think that good dancers are born, but all the good dancers I've ever met are taught or trained.

- Fred Astaire

Great dancers are great because of their passion.

-Martha Graham

The Great Secret of Tango

The great secret of Tango is the change of weight. You will always follow or lead better when you can implement the concept of split second weight shifting. The figures can change if you do not change the weight correctly. Here is a simple chart to make your weight change process much easier.

CHART FOR THE WEIGHT SHIFTING POSITIONS: LEADER

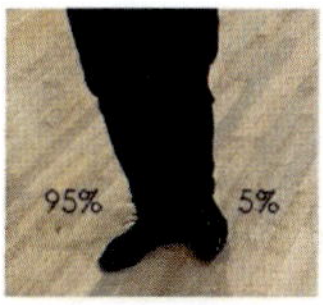

Standing position

Opening

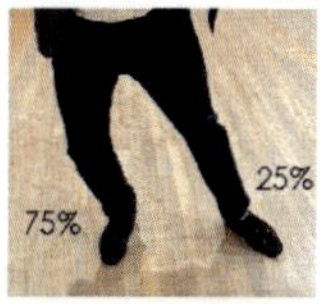

25% open

Transfer position to 75%

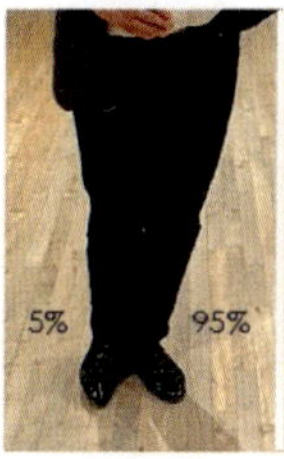

Collecting

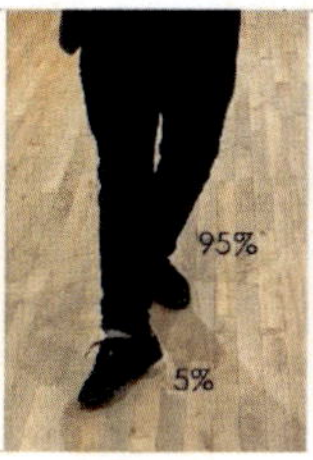

Projecting position

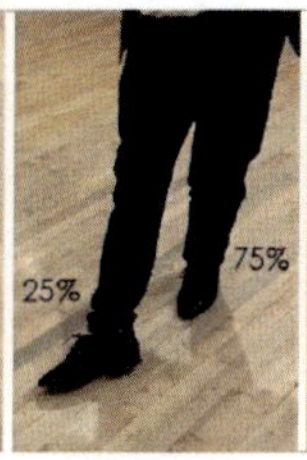

Extended position

Weight shifted to the front

Collecting position

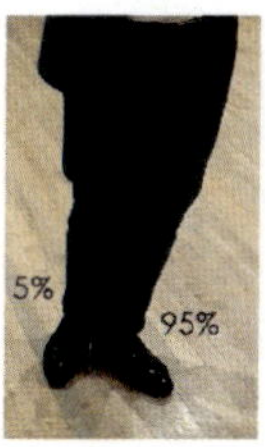

Collected position

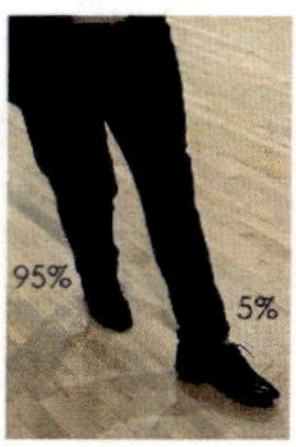

Extension position

Extended

Weight shifted standing position

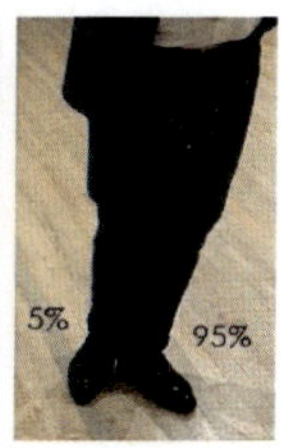

Collecting

Extended position

Weight shifted position

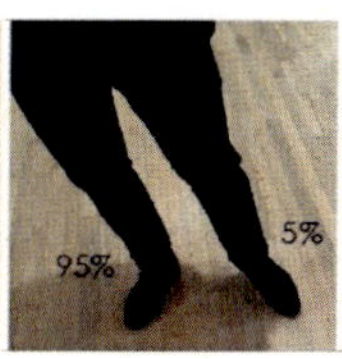

Collecting

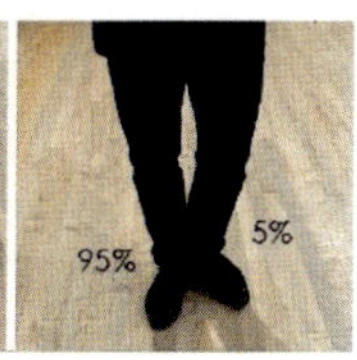

Collected

Basic Walk and Weight Shifting

1. Collect position: Left foot moves to the side with the inwardly rotated toe, transfers the weight and rotates the right inward, and collects.
2. go forward with the right foot, rotate the foot outside and extend the foot, transfer the weight and rotate the back foot inward and collect.
3. extend the same left leg and rotate outside, transfer the weight and rotate the right foot inward and collect. Settle down and put weight on both feet. Your feet together, and the girl is on the cross.
4. Rotate your left foot outside and extend the left leg, transfer the weight to the left and rotate the right foot inward and collect.

Open to the right with the same weight and inward rotate, transfer the weight, tilt the left inward and collect.

CHART FOR THE WEIGHT SHIFTING POSITIONS: FOLLOWER

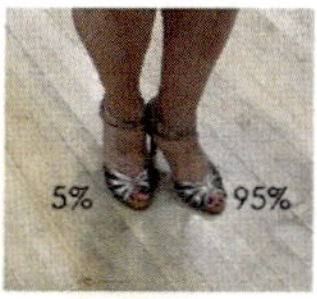

Standing position

Projecting position

Extended position

Weight shifted position

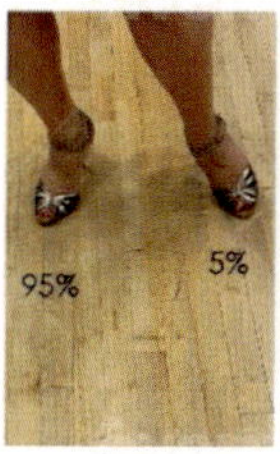

Collecting

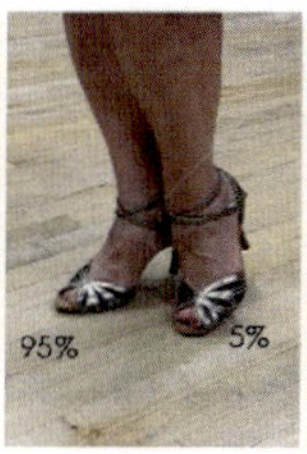

Collected position

Projecting position

Extended position

Weight shifted position

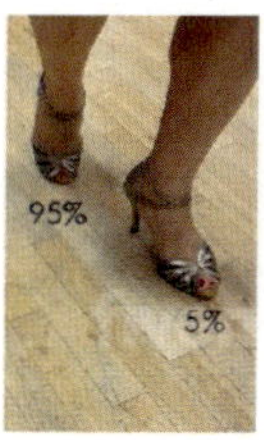

Collecting position

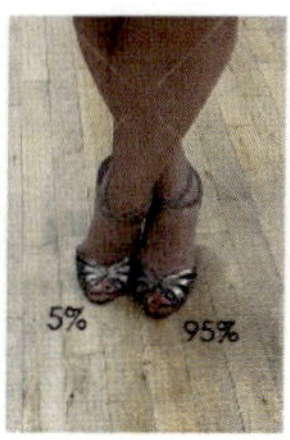

Cross position

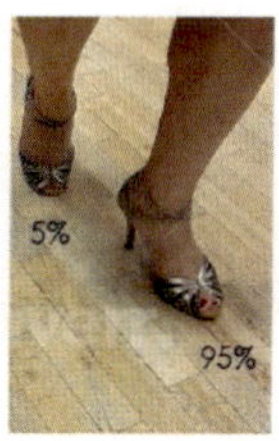

Projecting

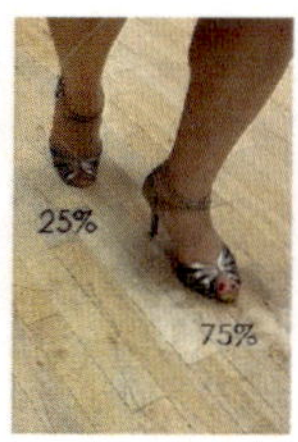

Extended

Weight shifted position

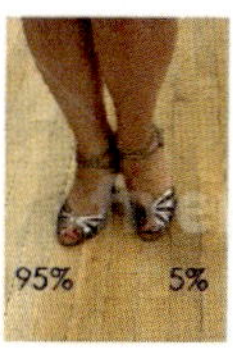

Collected position

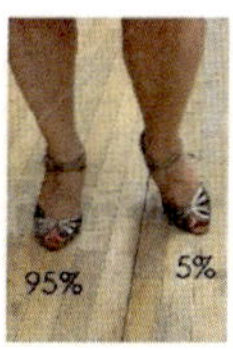

Projecting to the side

Extended position

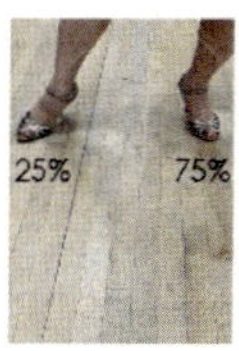

Weight shifted position

Collecting

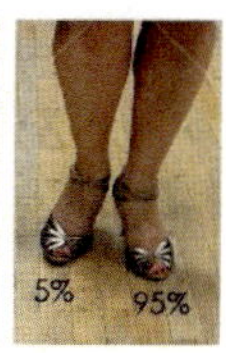

Collected

Basic Walk and Weight Shifting

1. Collect position: Right foot moves to the side and collect.
2. Turn the foot inward, rubbing the ankle and extending backward, and transfer the weight.
3. Turn the right out and glide it back and turn it inward to collect.
4. Extended to the back, turn left outward and do a cross.
5. Transfer the weight from the back to the front and extend the right foot to the back and the foot should be slightly rotated position.
6. Transfer weight and tilt the left foot outside and turn it inward to collect and keep it in the same position and extend to the side towards your left. Transfer the weight to the left and tilt the right foot inward and collect.

My teaching style is based on structure

A beginner student will work on their simple walking, cross-system, parallel system, terms, and simple weight shifting. As well as mini basic elements as described on my website, such as barridas, sacadas, gancho, baldosa, calesita, molinete, lapiz or rulo giro, ocho, sandwich, will work on perfecting their basic turns, and the most important is walking.

It is important for beginner dancers to understand how to move their frame properly and how to walk properly to avoid kicking their partner, yourself, or other dancers on the dance floor. Always be considerate of others and of yourself while on the floor.

Intermediate students will work on their intermediate steps. Parallel and cross system graceful walking and, adorno, firulete, calesita, apilada, bicicleta, colgata, corte, media luna, montesino, lustrada, enrosque, corrida or garavito, llevada arrastre, voleos, planeo, ocho cortado puente or carpa, sentada, volcada, and tijera or chilena. The intermediate boleos, barridas, back sacadas, and intermediate ganchos. Students will also learn to be ready to improvise with adding more intermediate levels steps.

It's very important and useful for Intermediate students to always refresh all their basic elements and to understand and accomplish in their intermediate levels journey.

Serious Tango dancers walk differently, feel differently, move differently, and process the music, the atmosphere, and the philosophy of tango differently, not only on the dance floor but in regular life as well. The passion for tango motivates them to feel better every day and makes them more sensitive and mindful in every aspect of life.

To be a good Tango dancer, you have to give nothing less than everything of yourself to it. It is a partnership and teamwork. This is when you realize that you cannot move your body on your own. In tango, you move when your partner moves. That can make it so difficult for some people so used to being in control. But that's one of the most attractive things I found in tango.

Technique is the grammar that holds the language of the dance together.

- Jon Tariq

Advanced dancers spend a lot of time learning combinations of steps, musicality, syncopation, and understanding different orchestra. They also learn to fully understand the proper way to dance the Tango, Milonga and Vals (waltz) and the difference between the stage tango and salon.

Refinements

The refinement starts when you enter a different level of your tango dancing. This doesn't mean that you've been dancing for 20 years, or you are from Argentina, so you are in a refinement position. No. After truly studying for a long time, you gain confidence to be able to do complex combinations totally effortlessly - this is when the refinement section starts.

If one doesn't study the Tango art technique, then what is there to refine? Just because you've been going to and hanging around different Milongas for 20+ years doesn't mean anything. You can still refine the things that you've been studying for years and years: all the techniques, the figures, the musicality, the moves, the certain beats and timing of certain music, etc. You cannot dance the same way all the time to different music.

Never underestimate how much your body can learn and how much you can do. This tremendous achievement comes after stepping into the refinement stage.

It's always important to set your goals so that someday you will get back the effort you put in. You will be more satisfied when you carry yourself with great pride, good technique, and full of better understanding than the others.

There will always be someone better than you. This doesn't mean you should stop working hard. Today may be their day, but tomorrow is yours if you continue your practice, study, and bring yourself up through the different levels.

The learning process never ends. You can't create a necklace if you don't first collect the stones and see what goes well with each other, each stone being a different tango technique.

On the dance floor, you don't rush. Listen to the music. Let it inspire and guide you across the dance floor. Let it connect you to your partner and create art together.

Someone is considered a good dancer when their technique is polished. Wearing expensive suits, skirts, and shoes can give you a good appearance, but it doesn't make you a good dancer.

You should dance every night or every week to practice, and for the fun of it. But you still need to take classes to learn the proper techniques. Anyone desiring to become a better dancer should take classes. Classes help you understand how to dance, how to lead, and how to follow. Tango instructors can show you your weaknesses and where you need to improve. Your teacher can show you things you could never see on your own. Make sure you find a teacher that you are comfortable with and who teaches according to your learning style. Every teacher has their own qualities. Make sure you find the right fit for you.

There is no magic number to how many classes you should take before you can say you're a good dancer. It is more determined by the quality of your practice. You get what you put in.

A dancer must learn when, how and what to do before attempting any adornment.

- Jon Tariq

There will always be someone a better dancer than you, but that does not mean that you will stop improving or leave your Obsession for Tango.

- Jon Tariq

Dance like the whole world is watching you.

- Jon Tariq

Chapter VIII

Learning the Tango lingo

Abrazo: (An embrace)

Aguja: (needle). A turn executed apparently on the point of the toe is usually done in conjunction with an enrosque.

Amague: (threatening motions-pretend) is used as an embellishment, either led or done on one's own, and may be used before taking a step.

Americana: a step where the leader pivots the follower to step through between the couple with the follower's left leg, and the leader pivots and steps through with the right leg. At that moment, the couple is Not in the mirror position, but at that time, they are facing in front in the same direction as an open book, the standing leg, which is the left of the guy in the standing leg, which is the right of the followers of the girl's leg left straight and the guys forward leg right straight that's we called Americana.

Andante: (walking at walking speed)

Andar: (to walk)

Apertura: (opening) In tango, an opening movement, often to the leader's left side.

Arrastrar: (to drag)

Arrastre: (drag)

Arriba: (up or upwards)

Atras: (back or backwards)

Apilado: (pile-up) dancing with full upper body contact. Apilado dancing is the way to increase the embrace's intimacy. It is most often used in the social tango scene and in Vals, and it can be done as a dance or as a pause.

Baldosa: (tile) short basic step, a square like a tile drawing the contour of the tile floor with one's foot. A square or box step. Any box step dancer will refer to Baldosa.

Barrida: (a sweep or a sweeping motion) One partner's foot sweeps the other's foot. Also called llevada.

Barrio: (a neighborhood)

Basic Salida: (Exit) Could be an opening or departure in a particular sequence of 6 steps. Any time we open to the left or to the right is the sidestep. Consider Salida. Also, a sequence of 6 or 8 Basic steps.

Bicicleta: (bike) simulating a bike pedal movement.

Boleo or Voleo: (throw) may be executed either high or low. Keeping knees together, with one leg in the back, swivel on the supporting leg. There are six types of Boleo: front lower boleo and back lower boleo, front upper boleo and back upper boleo, linear boleo, and cuantro boleo. To learn each one the proper way, you must ask your instructor or get help from a Tango professional.

Cadena: (sequence of steps)

Cadencia: (fancy walking)

Calesita: (carousel) The leader walks circularly around the follower, who pivots on one leg (or between two legs split axis) to stay connected with the leader as he circles her. Also called 'Molinete', a little mill.

Caminar: (walk) The walk on a dance floor and walking in the street are two different ideas.

The leg moves first, then the body follows. This is the proper way and If you follow this logic, you will always have a good balance.

Never lock the knees, or bend the knees. Always relax the knees. When you project the steps, and if the knees are relaxed, they will bend automatically as needed according to your extension of the step.

Walks should be practiced for balance and fluidity. The leg must extend before, and the upper frame follows after; what we call legs carry the body: 1-extend 2-transfer and 3- collect.

Carpa: (tent position) A figure created when the man leads the lady onto one foot as in, or at the end of, calesita and then steps back away from her, causing her to lean at an angle from her foot to his frame.

Castigada: (a punishment) When the leaders do a deeper sacada with his outside or inside thigh to the follower's outside tights, that creates an upper boleo and this move we call castigada.

Colgada: (hanged)

Colgadas: There are more than one ways to do Colgadas but here we have, the traditional (always together), the other is alternative (always lean outwards), and reverse leaning and rotating backward coming out.

In traditional colgadas, we spin to the left side of the leader and that is what we call *front colgada* and to the right of the leader, we do a *back colgada*. Both colgadas need to be connected.

You keep your frame straight and connect and the body stays straight nobody leans in any direction. Always keep your frame straight and knees relaxed, rotating on your own axis but make sure your frame stands straight no one is leaning to towards any side any direction. This traditional colgada you can do anywhere at any time.

Alternative colgadas: both leader and follower lean outwards, away from each other, out of their axis. They support each other from falling by maintaining their contact with their arms or stomach.

Alternative colgadas are not really comfortable on a crowded dance floor. You will always bump into someone.

Contragiros: (turns in the same direction)

Corrida: (a run) sequence of small and quick steps in a straight line.

Corte: (cut) A choreographic pause. In tango, corte means cutting the music by syncopating or holding several beats.

Cruce: (cross)

Cruzada: (cross) A cruzada occurs anytime a foot is crossed in front or in the back of the other.

Cunear: (to rock, cradle) A rocking movement, to and from.

Desplazamiento: (displacement) Displacing the partner's foot or leg using one's leg or foot.

Disociacion: (dissociation, disconnection) It refers to moving one part of the body independently of other parts.

Dibujo: (drawing, sketch) A dibujo is done by drawing circles or other small movements on the floor with one's toe.

Enganche: (hooking, coupling) Occurs when the partner wraps a leg around the other's leg. This is the wrap around and releases and going back to the same position from where the foot start. That's the right way.

Enrosque: (corkscrew) a twisting or corkscrew movement around one's vertical axis. Shoulders and hips remain parallel to the floor. A man's rotation. Pivoting on one foot while the other is tightly closed and crossed either in the front or in the back. While the woman executes a molinete, the man spins on one foot, hooking the other foot behind the spinning foot.

Entrada: (entrance) leader's leg replaces partner's unweighted leg position. Entrada doesn't influence the movement of the follower's leg. This movement is called entrada or sacada in Spanish, depending on the instructor and is often called a shallow sacada.

Espejo: (mirror) any position where the two people in the couple mirror each other.

Firulete: (an adornment, a decoration, an embellishment) Complicated or syncopated movements which the dancer uses to demonstrate their skill and to interpret the music.

Flecha: (arrow) In tango means make a shape like an arrowhead with one's feet.

Frenos: (brakes) To stop and hold.

Gancho: (leg hooks) A hooking move with the leg.

Giro: (turns) Circular movement or circular walk in which the follower satellites around the leader.

Lapiz: (pencil) A decoration in which the free foot draws a circle on the floor.

Lapiz/Rulo: (circular pencil) A circular drawing traced in the floor with the feet.

Llevada/Arrastre: (transport) The same as barrida.

Lustrada: (shoeshine) The follower gently runs the top of her foot up the leader's calf (this is not a lead but an optional decoration).

Marcar: (to mark, to indicate, to lead)

Media Luna: (half-moon) A turn. The woman turns 180 degrees around the man.

Media Vuelta: (half turn) Usually done when the man's right foot and the woman's left foot are free. Media Vuelta is used by itself to change direction or maneuver on the dance floor and as an entrance to many combinations. Also, it's good to do the leader's left foot back in the fall. Right foot back when you rotate, you are automatically in the proposition of 1, and if the six-count then is the 2nd stop is 2 and walk forward 3 and 4 to the cross.

Milonga: may refer to music, the dance and the place where we dance the tango.

Milongueros: refers to those frequenting or those who spend time dancing at socials (at Milongas).

Molinetes: forward and backward ochos (figure 8's) done in a circle. It can be 4, 8, or 12, and the last advanced way for the professional or advanced dancers is counting 3.

Mordida: (a bite) Same meaning as a sandwich.

Ocho: (eight) Figure eights are usually executed with feet together (ankles touching) instead of one foot extended.

Ocho atras: (backward eights)

Ocho Cortado: (cut eights) A figure eight cut in half. My favorite step is always a helpful step on the dance floor.

Parada: (stop) In this movement, the follower is brought to a standstill, usually with at least one foot touching the leader's extended free foot.

Pasada: (passing over) This is where the leader invites the follower to step over his leg following a parada or sandwich. The lady may, at her discretion, step over the man's foot or trace her toe on the floor around its front.

Patada: (kick)

Pista: (dance floor)

Planeo: (glade)A movement performed by the leader, or led by the follower, that uses momentum to cause the free foot to create a wide arc on the floor as the dancer turns. The two legs resemble a pair of compasses drawing a circle, with the free foot the pencil pivoting one. On the bent leg, the dancer rotates on his axis, keeping the other leg straight.

Planeo is also called in English, airplane. Some teachers will refer to that.

Puente/Carpa: (bridge/tent) An action in which the man pulls the woman to himself by taking her out of her axis.

Punteo: (plucking)A decoration where you tap the floor with the point of your foot. Varying from little taps low to the ground or in such a way that the leg bounces high off the ground afterwards.

Quebradas: (brakes)

Rulo: (a curl) A decoration. Also known as lapiz or dibujo, a rulo is executed by drawing one or more circles on the floor with the free leg, either as part of a movement or during a pause in dancing.

Sacadas: (displacements) The displacement of the partner's unweighted leg.

Salida: (exit or start) A place to start or to get out of a figure. Any time we open to the left or to the right is the sidestep and it is considered a salida. Also, a sequence of 6 basic steps or can be basic of 8 counts or just walk BASIC we open Salida for all of those.

Salida cruzada: (the beginning of a pattern with a cross). *Also, called* Basic Cruzada or a six 6 count basic step.

Leader: open salida with the left and collect -1
Walking forward with the right leg outside partner -2
Step forward with the left- 3
Collect –feet together (when the girl is on a cross)-4
Step forward with the left and collect -5
Open to the right and collect-6

Follower: side right and collect -1
Walking back with the left -2
Walking back with the right -3
Crossing left on top of right - 4.
Walking back to the right and collecting that 5
Opening to the side with the left and collect 6

Sandwich/sandwichito: (sandwich) One partner's foot is sandwiched or trapped between the other partner's feet. Also known as mordida.

Sentada: (sit) Woman sitting on the man's leg.

Soltada: (released) a move where the couple temporarily let go of each other.

Tijra/Chilena: (scissors) A small jump with scissoring steps in between the partner's legs.

Trabada: (fastened) It is a lock step - the step that the woman takes when the man steps outside with his right foot and then straight forward left, together right. At this point, the woman crosses (this cross is referred to as trabada). Also called cruzada.

Traspie: (trip)

Volcada: (dunk/hang) a move which involves the follower deliberately going off her axis and leaning towards her partner, who sustains her and prevents her from falling.

Voleo: whipping action of one leg over the other in the front and back. It requires a close interaction between leader and follower for successful and perfect timing and execution.

Smoother: means lovers can be done on the front or back and Whipping action stronger it's either for the front or back.

A dancer must learn when, how, and what to do before attempting any adornment.

- Jon Tariq

I feel rewarded, when my student dances gracefully.

-Jon Tariq

Chapter IX

Tango Dress Etiquette

Tango outfits are mostly black, combined with sad music and mystic atmosphere to evoke seriousness. Red is also used by a woman and it is associated with love, passion, sex, speed on the dance floor, and aggressiveness. In Tango, the points of attraction are the high heels. They are considered a symbol of playful defiance, bringing attention to the legs and making them look sexy and seductive. Fishnet stockings conceal and reveal at once. Traditionally professional dancers wear the regular fishnet with a medium-sized diamond pattern, but some like the wider diamond pattern to be racier. All these combined give an illusion of a teasing seduction.

Women

<u>Nylons and fishnet stockings</u>: Not everyone likes to wear them during social events, but you will see that some women will wear them to every event. I won't

recommend liquid stockings since that can ruin the men's trousers. If you want the color without the mess, try tanning instead.

Tango shoes: are stiletto shoes approximately 3″ to 4″ high. If you are buying your first pair of tango shoes and you are not used to wearing heels, then a low heel is the best option for you until you develop your balance.

When purchasing tango shoes, you don't want a lot of room between the end of your toes and the end of the shoe. If your toes are quite close to the edge, this is ok.
Most brands have a chart with the size and length of their shoes. Always measure your feet and compare them against the chart. If still in doubt, don't hesitate to ask the shoe company for help.

Most companies will suggest choosing a closed heel, meaning that the back of your feet is supported and strapped into the shoe. This is great for first-timers as it helps with balance and makes you feel more secure. And, as a rule of thumb, snug shoes will stretch and mold to your feet; shoes that dent, cut into your skin, or hurt the first time you try them on, will only give you pain. Shoes that are "roomy" and fit comfortably loose straight away will probably start slipping off. Choose shoes based on looks and comfort.

Dresses: In the past, long dresses were worn, but today any dress that can flow fluently will do. However, there are Tango-specific dresses with front, side, and/or back splits, and fishtails made with all skirt lengths and styles.

Men

Tango shoes: Comfortable and flexible leather or other material. Rounded toes are a must; otherwise, they'd get in the way. Leather or suede soles that will let you slide and pivot. Low heel.

Trousers: Never with cuffs because heels can get caught.

If you like, wear suits, and vests. It will make you look sharp.

Dress to impress! What is more beautiful and sexier than the Argentine tango? Remember, appearance is very important, since you are going to see yourself with your dance partner and with the others with whom you dance on the floor.

–Jon Tariq

Chapter X

It takes two to tango

This phrase originated from the dancing tango, which requires two partners to perform. This phrase gained popularity in 1952 with the song Takes Two to Tango by Al Hoffman and Dick Manning. It was a cultural success, integrating the saying into popular culture as a way to say it takes to people to enjoy something.

The "tango" in the saying refers to an activity that two people need to participate in together to make it work. The phrase can have positive or negative connotations, depending on the situation.

"It takes two to Tango" is an idiomatic expression used a lot today to emphasize that it takes two people working collaboratively with another person who are willing to take part in something to make it happen to achieve a common goal. It is a team effort, and each partner is equally responsible, and the combined efforts make for a better outcome.

People use this phrase to express they need assistance with something. It could also be used like this: So you think you can do this all alone? I have news for you, it takes two to tango. You could do lots of things alone, but as the song says, darling, it always takes two to Tango.

"It takes two to tango"; one dictates the steps, and the other executes them effectively. That is how a great show is made.

- Olaotan Fawehinmi

Chapter XI

The Perfect Stranger

The perfect stranger is the partner you are looking for to get practice outside your dance lessons to review and perfect your moves.

This is the section where I answer the question I am asked every day: Where do I find a dance partner?

1. You can find a partner in your weekly or monthly Milongas or
2. In my website. There you'll find a link: **Dance Partner Search** registration form. Fill out the criteria you are looking for and we will match you with someone.

But before you try to find a dance partner, have a clear understanding of what your ambitious and goals are and what you want to get out of the partnership. It is also the time for your stranger, a future dance partner, to see if you are a good match for him/her.

Remember that it is extremely important to continue your lessons so you can correct your mistakes and improve your technique and more as a couple. Everyone should have an instructor if they want to grow.

So You Have a Match

Let's say you found that perfect stranger. Now ask yourself:

1. Do you share the same goals?
2. How is their personality? Personality doesn't change. So make sure you can accept the person as what they are.
3. Do they make you feel at ease? If you are at ease, you are feeling confident and relaxed,
4. Take into consideration your own body and your personal preferences. Think about whether you will need to be able to lift or hold yourself.
5. How committed are they?
6. Did you discuss how often do you want to meet?
7. Find a partner close to your goals.
8. Give it a trail. Sometimes you will find positive and negative surprises

Then this is when you try your best to be respectful and cultivate the relationship so the perfect stranger and you can have a future together.

1. Hygiene is important
2. Be respectful. Never rude or critical
3. Always keep your word. This means being dependable
4. Do not try to impress your partner or outshine your partner with your elevated dance skills. It will only make you look bad. Argentine Tango is primary. The leader leads, and the follower follows.
5. Loyalty. You need a partner that is loyal to the partnership. Question to ask: "How many partners have you had and what was the reason you broke up?
6. Communicate. This will show how far you will go with this person.
7. Have faith
8. Be positive

Now what?

Go dance and Remember, It Takes Two to Tango.

Chapter XII

Should I take a flight to Buenos Aires?

Absolutely, taking a flight to Buenos Aires promises an enchanting journey into the heart of tango, a dance that resonates with the very pulse of Argentina. This captivating art form beckons travelers globally to immerse themselves in its passionate embrace.

For those yearning for an authentic tango experience, Buenos Aires, the vibrant capital, stands as a haven. Tango-themed hotels not only provide comfortable lodgings but also serve as lively hubs for daily tango lessons and themed dance rooms. Suites with private dance floors cater to enthusiastic dancers eager to refine their moves in the privacy of their accommodations.

Buenos Aires doesn't merely host tango; it lives and breathes it. The city resonates with captivating tango shows and milongas, creating an atmosphere where one might feel an insatiable appetite for all things tango. To truly grasp the richness of the tango community, engaging with locals and seeking out the numerous milongas scattered across the city is essential. These social dance gatherings offer more than rhythmic movements; they provide a gateway to the vibrant tango culture.

For those venturing into this passionate world, staying informed about travel advisories is crucial, ensuring a safe and enjoyable exploration of Argentina's tango scene. The Travel State.gov website (https://travel.state.gov/content/travel.html) serves as a valuable resource for up-to-date information. Travelers should be aware of the importance of exercising precautions and paying attention to cultural differences, such as the tradition of meeting strangers for coffee after a milonga, which might signify an invitation for a more intimate connection.

Understanding and respecting tango codes (códigos) and traditions, coupled with maintaining good manners during the visit to Argentina, ensures a seamless and enriching experience. The beauty of it all is that you don't need to speak spanish to savor the adventure; simply let the universal language of tango guide your steps and enjoy the captivating journey in Argentina will do just fine! You don’t need to speak spanish to visit Argentina. Just enjoy the adventure!

Chapter XIII

The maestro Jon Tariq reflecting on his life in tango

The teacher Jon Tariq answering the question of what does he do and why?

I am a Tango instructor and that is all I do. Tango is my life, my joy and my bread and butter, but tango is more than that. Every day I teach people to tango. It may sound easy, but it's not as simple as it seems. Practice requires effort. Doing any activity for hours at a time is strenuous and exhausting. So many little things that happen that influence the dance student in a way that one never knows or realizes, but in the end it's all worth it, because every moment where one makes the effort to teach a student to practice it, will make them then do better and better.

When a student comes to me to learn tango at any level, I have a sense of responsibility and a sense of obligation, and it is a privilege to teach someone who chooses me as their teacher. So I take my role as an instructor very seriously.

My dance studio is an attractive environment for them to improve their skills and prepare to achieve their goals.
I give my students the attention and patience they deserve, as this plays an important role in their success in their tango career. I listen to their needs and wants and watch their adaptability as they learn and this is where differentiation in terms of mode of instruction and content comes into play. This will help me make the learning process more personalized to improve student self-esteem and self-awareness, the two important ingredients for student success.

I always dance with my students when I see them in my milongas, or in any other milonga. It gives me joy and great pleasure to dance with them because they are part of my life. This also gives me a chance to feel where they are and it will give me an idea of where they need to improve.

I admire all students when they put in effort and it's fascinating to see some of them walk so smoothly. I love seeing their dynamics as they move down the track. It is inspiring for others too.

I share all the technique with my students. The information I learned by myself or from my teachers, from hard work and years and years of training so that I could see my students prosper.

Jon tells us that the moment his students start doing the tango walk is like a baby's first steps.

When my students manage to maintain their balance and take their first steps it is like the first steps of a baby. You are watching every second and get excited when they achieve any move successfully.
Let's be real for a minute: some dancers spend a lot of time tangoing, but they know absolutely only a little

about how they should dance. They need an instructor to correct them, so it's normal for teachers to take delight in our students, even with the slightest achievement. Hold their foot to show them correct technique or see when they can stand upright on their own, or just feel the music; all worth celebrating. However, among the most exciting (and memorable) milestones are the dancer's first steps: tango walks. It is easy to see that often a small step for a beginning dancer it's a big leap for an instructor.

When a student takes their first step, it's the same feeling as a parent with a child: steps can vary wildly from one dancer to another, even within the same student level. Some learn faster than others, but in the end it's also about the time invested. A good rule of thumb is not to compare your student to others.

Student progress in a predictable sequence. They start out simple, then move on to more complex steps. Before taking their first steps, for example, they learn to maintain balance, coordination, agility and to stay upright. As they trust the dancer, they learn more precise movements.

Teachers want to be great teachers over time because when our students look great, so do we. I always try to transmit the passion I have for tango to my students, since they already have some passion for tango. Their passion grows as they get better at their dancing and then it becomes an obsession. It's fascinating to see progress and I'm lucky enough to experience it every day of my life and look forward to continuing to do so.

My teaching experience has brought me to a point where I can appreciate the little things in life. My focus and attention is what nourishes and sustains me in life and brings me even the smallest amount of pleasure without taking things for granted, and I am grateful for that. I am very happy with my life and I do my best every day to give my students the best education they deserve. This is what I do and why I do it. It's worth getting up every day and sharing my world with those who care.

Conclusion

When you dance the tango, you become sensitive to your partner's signals for a 3-minute dance. Your body is full of exciting energy, and you want to do it all over again and again. You feel alive and happy. If you have a passion, then you also have an obsession.

Tango is just like any other skill you try to develop. You have to put in the effort and the time to build a solid foundation and be able to stand the repeated structure and perfection will come from repetition and what type of skill this person has developed.

The basic elements of Argentine Tango are the embrace, walking, figures, dancing patterns and the type of music playing, whether it is a traditional Tango, a Milonga, or a Vals.

At every level of your Tango journey, learn to analyze the main structure of the Tango music. Recognize the layers, follow specific music instruments, and improvise to various rhythms. Study the musical masters. There is always more learning to do.

Understanding musicality is extremely important nowadays because of Tango music's evolution. Simply feeling the music and listening to the music is not enough anymore.

The key to becoming a great tango dancer lies within you. You have to spend the time to get better, have the strength and determination to pursue your goals and believe in yourself. Never stop learning and continue your Tango journey.

On the dance floor, be open-minded to many ideas, and possibilities, and it is very important to connect with your partner at that moment.

At the same time, disconnect yourself from everything that occupies your mind and be free.

You should not rush. Slow down, and share with your partner that beautiful feeling and indescribable moment that you are going through.

Tango is teamwork. If they think that they are better than the other, they will never enjoy or look good dancing together at that moment.

The Secret of tango dancing is to bring down yourself to the level of the person you agreed to dance with. It's never about one can show themselves without the other in a beautiful manner. The only time you will look amazing together is when you detach yourself from these types of thoughts, feelings and ideas. At the end, it's not about how good you are. It's all about how good you can dance with that person. And don't forget that it takes two to tango. One can't do anything alone in tango; that's the beauty of tango partnership.

Remember, you're not there to get something. You are there to give everything like a true Tangero. Celebrate every single beat with your dance partner among other dancers on the dance floor.

The passion, desire, and the strong and barely uncontrollable emotion you feel when you dance tango is what I call the tango obsession. I love tango.

If you've ever wanted to learn to tango, why not take the first step? I'm here to help you navigate your journey. Let's dance into the world of tango together!

Jon Tariq

NY Tango School

https://tangoschool.nyc/jon-tariq/

Historical References:

A book called Lucanba by Gustavo Goldman shows proofs of the relationship between social, cultural, historical and musical. 1870-1890.

El Tango en la Sociedad Portena 1880-1920 by Hugo Lamas chronologically shows the Tango life.
Las Raíces Del Tango-Cronología (Eduardo Giorlandini 1820-1825)

The investigations of "El Nacimiento y Evolución de los Estilos en el tango" The birth and the evolution of the styles of Tango by Cesar Lorenz from the UNTREF (Universidad Nacional Tres De Febrero)2018

Gabriela Nouzeilles, Graciela R. Montaldo (2002). The Argentina Reader: History, Culture, Politics. Duke University Press. pp. 197–198. ISBN 0-8223-2914-X. tango etymology.

Diccionario del Español Actua(Conde, 2013): Definitition of Jerga popular, originariamente de maleantes, típica de Buenos Aires y extendida por los países de la Plata (Manuel Seco-Olimpia-Ramos 1999: 2.891).

Viejo Tanguero. Publisher: Buenos Aires : Club de Tango, 1995

Pasado y presente de los negros en Buenos Aires Juan Carlos Coria Editorial J.A. Roca, 1997
Tango de la casera" (Oliver Buesa, 1987)

Tango: discusión y clave. Con una antología de informaciones y opiniones sobre el tango y su mundo (Sábato, Ernesto R 1968) (Sergio Alejandro Pujol ·1999)

Candombe ; Juan Antonio Varese; Tomás Olivera Chirimini · Montevideo, Uruguay (Banda Oriental 2018)

La música y la danza de los negros en el Buenos Aires de los siglos XVIII y XIX. (Ricardo E Rodríguez Molas)

Tango: the art history of love (Robert Farris Thompson)

Koelsch S (2014) Brain correlates of music-evokes emotions Nat Rev Neirosci 20 fevr 15 (3): nrn 3666

Mas-Herrero E, Zatorre RJ, Rodriguez-Fornells A, Marco-Pallares J (2014) Dissociation between Musical and Monetary Rewards Responses in Specific Music Anhedonia

Tango Music is ranked among the highest sources of pleasure. Alsaleh MA. Benefits of Argentine Tango in Diseases and Disorders. Psychol Behav Sci Int J. 2019

Tango Masters collection and Tango Stories: Musical Secrets, the guide to tango dance music by Michael Lavocah

Understanding Musicality: "Al Compás del Corazón" and Advanced Musicality Secrets of Success: Filling in the Blanks of Argentine Tango by Oliver Kent PhD

Let's dance to the music by Joaquín Amenábar

Todo Tango –historia -Orquesta-Tipica-Juan-DArienzo

Wikipedia "Juan d'Arienzo"

Tango Stories: Musical Secrets" by Michael Lavocah

Tango en el Espejo, "Pensalo Bien"

Very tango store -legends-juan-darienzo

Los Estílos Fundamentales del Tango Ignacio Varchausky

Hidden History of Tango By Denniston, Christine

UNESCO's Living Heritage Entity.

Crónica general del tango", José Gobello, Editorial Fraterna, 1980.

"El tango", Horacio Salas, Editorial Aguilar, 1996.

"Historia del tango - La Guardia Vieja", Rubén Pesce, Oscar del Priore, Silvestre Byron, Editorial Corregidor 1977.

El tango, el gaucho y Buenos Aires", Carlos Troncaro, Editorial Argenta, 2009.